FLOWERS FOR MRS HOPKINS

by Gladys M. Hogg

SAMUEL FRENCH

Copyright © 1983 by Samuel French Ltd
All Rights Reserved

FLOWERS FOR MRS HOPKINS is fully protected under the copyright laws of the British Commonwealth, including Canada, the United States of America, and all other countries of the Copyright Union. All rights, including professional and amateur stage productions, recitation, lecturing, public reading, motion picture, radio broadcasting, television, online/digital production, and the rights of translation into foreign languages are strictly reserved.

ISBN 978-0-573-13239-1
concordtheatricals.co.uk
concordtheatricals.com

FOR AMATEUR PRODUCTION ENQUIRIES

UNITED KINGDOM AND WORLD
EXCLUDING NORTH AMERICA
licensing@concordtheatricals.co.uk
020-7054-7200

Each title is subject to availability from Concord Theatricals, depending upon country of performance.

CAUTION: Professional and amateur producers are hereby warned that *FLOWERS FOR MRS HOPKINS* is subject to a licensing fee. The purchase, renting, lending or use of this book does not constitute a licence to perform this title(s), which licence must be obtained from the appropriate agent prior to any performance. Performance of this title(s) without a licence is a violation of copyright law and may subject the producer and/or presenter of such performances to penalties. Both amateurs and professionals considering a production are strongly advised to apply to the appropriate agent before starting rehearsals, advertising, or booking a theatre. A licensing fee must be paid whether the title is presented for charity or gain and whether or not admission is charged.

This work is published by Samuel French, an imprint of Concord Theatricals Ltd.

The Professional Rights in this play are controlled by Aldwych House, 71-91 Aldwych, London, WC2B 4HN, UK.

No one shall make any changes in this title for the purpose of production. No part of this book may be reproduced, stored in a retrieval system, scanned, uploaded, or transmitted in any form, by any means, now known or yet to be invented, including mechanical, electronic, digital, photocopying, recording, videotaping, or otherwise, without the prior written permission of the publisher. No one shall share this title, or part of this title, to any social media or file hosting websites.

The moral right of Gladys M. Hogg to be identified as author of this work has been asserted in accordance with Section 77 of the Copyright, Designs and Patents Act 1988.

USE OF COPYRIGHTED MUSIC

A licence issued by Concord Theatricals to perform this play does not include permission to use the incidental music specified in this publication. In the United Kingdom: Where the place of performance is already licensed by the PERFORMING RIGHT SOCIETY (PRS) a return of the music used must be made to them. If the place of performance is not so licensed then application should be made to PRS for Music (www.prsformusic.com). A separate and additional licence from PHONOGRAPHIC PERFORMANCE LTD (www.ppluk.com) may be needed whenever commercial recordings are used. Outside the United Kingdom: Please contact the appropriate music licensing authority in your territory for the rights to any incidental music.

USE OF COPYRIGHTED THIRD-PARTY MATERIALS

Licensees are solely responsible for obtaining formal written permission from copyright owners to use copyrighted third-party materials (e.g., artworks, logos) in the performance of this play and are strongly cautioned to do so. If no such permission is obtained by the licensee, then the licensee must use only original materials that the licensee owns and controls. Licensees are solely responsible and liable for clearances of all third-party copyrighted materials, and shall indemnify the copyright owners of the play(s) and their licensing agent, Concord Theatricals Ltd., against any costs, expenses, losses and liabilities arising from the use of such copyrighted third-party materials by licensees.

IMPORTANT BILLING AND CREDIT REQUIREMENTS

If you have obtained performance rights to this title, please refer to your licensing agreement for important billing and credit requirements.

CHARACTERS

Mrs Hopkins
Jane Adams, her married daughter
Postie
Visitor

The action takes place in the living-room of Mrs Hopkins' ground-floor flat

Time — the present

PRODUCTION NOTE

The tape-recording of the two children plays a very important part in either complementing or providing sharp contrast to the action. It is imperative that the children's voices do not sound contrived and for the original production the tape which was finally used was the one made when the children were unaware that they were being recorded. Mrs Hopkins switches on the tape three times but there is no wind-back so the children's voices must be continuous with much laughter, singing and childish chattering.

To my husband, Charles;
Sandy Mitchell; Derek Horn (Adjudicator)
and the Selkirk Players

FLOWERS FOR MRS HOPKINS

The living-room of Mrs Hopkins' ground-floor flat

There is a door UCL which leads into the hall, which has a front door R. An archway, UR leads to the kitchen. The furniture consists of a bookcase, on which stand framed photographs of children, a sideboard, a dining-table, three chairs and an easy chair. DR is an armchair with a trolley to the side of it, on which stands the phone and a tape-recorder. On the lower shelf of the trolley is a phone-pad and various magazines and papers

When the CURTAIN rises Mrs Hopkins enters from the kitchen. She is a bright, independent old lady of eighty-one, who does not wish to become a burden on her family and has taken steps to make sure that does not happen. Slightly disabled, she walks with a stick and is pushing, with difficulty, a hoover. She is wearing a cardigan buttoned-up wrongly and a duster hangs from her pocket. She leaves the hoover and dusts around, humming to herself. Then she hangs the stick on the back of the chair, puts the duster in her pocket, plugs in the hoover and starts hoovering the carpet

Jane Adams enters from the hall, in outdoor clothes, carrying a shopping-basket and a plate covered with foil. She is Mrs Hopkins' daughter; in her forties. House-proud and always in a hurry, she is well intentioned and genuinely concerned for her mother. Worried by her mother's activities, she quickly puts the shopping basket and plate on the table and switches off the hoover at the main

Mrs Hopkins Oh, Jane, it's you ...
Jane Mother, how many more times must I tell you? (*Unplugging the hoover and winding the flex*) What is the point of my coming here every morning if you insist on doing everything for yourself? (*She pushes the hoover away*)
Mrs Hopkins I was just ...
Jane (*taking the stick from the chair and handing it to her mother*) It's dangerous, don't you see? (*Taking the duster from Mrs Hopkins' pocket and handing it to her*) Dusting—yes,

hoovering—no. And just look at you—all in a muddle. (*She rebuttons Mrs Hopkins' cardigan in the correct fashion and turns back her cuffs*) There now, that's better. (*She removes her own coat and puts it on a chair, then she takes the biscuits from her basket to a tin on the bookcase*)

Mrs Hopkins (*dusting the table*) I was just trying to help, dear. You do like everything to be so perfect. And, well, with your job at the office, and Jim and the children and everything. It's—it's just too much for you, Jane. I don't want to be a burden——

Jane (*exasperatedly*) You are not a burden, Mother. (*Taking the duster from Mrs Hopkins; more kindly*) How many more times must I tell you that? But you must help me to help you.

Mrs Hopkins (*wiping her nose with a handkerchief*) I do try, dear, honestly I do. But I get worried.

Jane About what?

Mrs Hopkins About getting—well, you know—really old. At not being able to do anything for myself. At becoming a complete burden on you ...

Jane Oh no, not that again. (*She goes to the table, takes the newspaper, parcel and tape from the basket and leaves them on the table with the covered plate. She takes the basket to the sideboard*) You distress yourself and me when you go on like that ...

Jane takes the cups and saucers from out of the sideboard and cutlery and paper table napkins from the drawer. She leaves them all on the top of the sideboard and stays busy as Mrs Hopkins speaks—she has heard it all before and has no wish to hear it again

Mrs Hopkins I—I just couldn't bear it, Jane. Not to be able to use my own hands. To be spoon fed. To be brushed and patted like a newly-made hospital bed. My brain—it could be alive, but my body—dead. I might—I might not even be able to talk. I could even wet the bed. (*She recoils at the thought*) No, no, I couldn't stand that. (*Calmer now, she sits in her armchair*)

Jane takes the cups and saucers and napkins to the table

(*Looking at Jane*) When the time comes, I shall do what I have to do. Y—you won't stop me, will you, Jane? I shall just sit in my chair, close my eyes, and go to sleep. Quite peacefully ... Y—you will understand, won't you, dear?

Jane picks up the foil-covered plate and approaches Mrs Hopkins

Jane (*kindly*) Enough of that, Mother. With all this nonsense we've forgotten what day it is! (*She lifts the foil from the plate to reveal a birthday cake with one candle*) Voilà! Happy birthday, Mum. (*She kisses Mrs Hopkins*)

Mrs Hopkins Oh, it's beautiful. Thank you, Jane.

Jane returns the cake to the table and then, during the following, takes the tape and parcel to Mrs Hopkins

In the midst of everything—you remembered. Er, what am I, eighty-two or eighty-three?

Jane You're eighty-one, just a chicken. (*She hands over the tape and parcel*) That's from Jim and me, and the girls made the tape last night. More giggles than greetings, I'm afraid.

Jane hurriedly checks her watch and then goes and sets out the cups and saucers on the table and generally tidies up while Mrs Hopkins opens her parcel

Mrs Hopkins (*scattering paper and string on the floor*) A cardigan, just what I needed ...

Jane (*pushing the hoover to the kitchen archway*) I thought you'd like it. Hope it fits. (*She gets her basket from the sideboard*)

Jane exits to the kitchen, taking the hoover and basket with her

Mrs Hopkins And chocolates, mm, soft centres, bet that was the children's idea. Buy Granny chocolates and no prizes for guessing who'll eat most of them. Bless 'em. (*She opens two envelopes enclosed in the parcel*)

Jane enters from the kitchen with the empty basket and a jug of water. She puts the jug on a tray on the sideboard and the basket on the chair with her coat

Jane (*going to Mrs Hopkins*) The girls will be round straight from school, Mum—about four. Don't worry about them. They know to watch the roads.

We hear the sound of whistling. The doorbell rings

That'll be your friend the Postie.

Mrs Hopkins (*rising excitedly, dropping her presents*) A whistling woman, a crowing hen, is neither fit for God nor men! Don't tell her I said that, she won't give me my letters.

Jane (*laughing*) Honestly, Mum, you're worse than a child. Just look at all that mess. (*She picks up the string*) Anyway, how do you know you will get any more letters?

The doorbell rings again

Postie (*off*) Coo-ee, Mrs Hopkins ...
Jane I'll go. (*She goes to the hall, still carrying the string, leaving the door open. She opens the front door*)

Jane, still visible, talks to the Postie off, but their conversation is inaudible. Mrs Hopkins picks up her presents and puts them on the trolley

Mrs Hopkins (*sitting again*) Just listen to them. All that time for chattering. (*Shouting*) What's going on out there? I want my letters ...
Jane (*to Postie*) Well, just for a moment. (*She comes back to the living-room, looking concerned and thoughtfully winding the string*)

Postie enters carrying a mail bag and closes the door behind her. She is in her twenties, tarty, cheeky and inefficient but she likes Mrs Hopkins if only for a gossip. Jane tolerates her for her mother's sake

Postie (*ignoring Jane*) Happy birthday, Mrs Hopkins. (*She throws her bag on to a chair*)
Mrs Hopkins (*putting on her glasses*) Morning, Postie. Well, come on, what have you got for me?
Postie (*looking in her bag*) Now, let's have a look. (*Taking out a pile of letters*) Eh, bills, bills, bills. We don't want those, do we? Ah, here we are. Mrs Hopkins, Mrs Hopkins and Mrs Hopkins. (*She gives Mrs Hopkins the letters*) There now, and oh, I nearly forgot. (*She looks in the bag again*) This one's from me. (*She hands her a parcel*) And that's your lot. What's it feel like to be twenty-one?

Agitated, Jane looks at her watch and folds the paper napkins on the table

Mrs Hopkins Cheeky. (*Opening the parcel*) Jane tells me I'm eighty-one, but I can never remember. (*More paper and string*

Flowers for Mrs Hopkins

falls to the floor) Soap, oh how kind. It smells lovely. *(She opens the card)*

Postie Lavender. *(Whispering to Jane)* My aunty gave it to me for Christmas. Thought it was more her than me, if you know what I mean. *(Giggling)* Whew! I'm late this morning. What a carry on. I was just telling your daughter ...

Jane picks up the scattered paper and puts it in the waste-bin

Jane *(looking at her watch)* You'll be even later if you don't watch your time ...

Mrs Hopkins What were you telling my daughter?

Postie About that woman that's still on the run. Did you not hear it on the radio? They say she's a——

Jane *(going to the door and willing Postie to leave)* No need for details. They'll soon pick her up.

Postie *(expansively)* They say she's quite mad. She's a psycho — psycho — something. That means she's dangerous. The police have warned the public not to approach her. So don't you go——

Jane *(coughing and opening the door wide)* Thank you and goodmorning.

Postie *(ignoring Jane)* So just you watch it, Mrs Hopkins. She's been seen in this area. Not even got a coat on. Just a blue cotton dress ...

Mrs Hopkins Poor soul. In this weather too.

Jane *(taking Postie by the arm)* Thank you and *goodbye*.

Postie *(mistaking it for a friendly "goodbye")* Oh, cheerio, Mrs Adams. *(Grabbing her bag from the chair)* Nice to have had a chat. And happy birthday again, Mrs Hopkins. *(Still talking as she is escorted out)* So just you remember what I said now, don't you ...

Jane and Postie exit

Mrs Hopkins *(overlapping Postie's last words)* Bye, Postie, and thank you ... *(She opens all the cards and throws the envelopes to the floor)*

Jane enters. She is distressed and annoyed

Jane Really, Mother, you should not encourage that female, she's a menace.

Mrs Hopkins What was she on about anyway?

Jane (*sighing and putting the dropped envelopes in the wastebin*) Nothing for you to worry about. You know how she does go on. I'm sure the police will have the situation well in hand. What's this? (*Taking a man's cap from under the chair*) It's a man's cap! Where did it come from?

Mrs Hopkins (*guiltily*) How should I know?

Jane Well it's not Jim's. He never wears a cap. Mother, what have you been up to?

Mrs Hopkins N—nothing, dear—I——

Jane Mother! Who's been here?

Mrs Hopkins It was the—er—man to read the meter.

Jane But the meter's in the hall.

Mrs Hopkins Well, yes, but I—er—had just made some tea, and he was cold. So, I asked him in for a cuppa. He loved your shortbread, dear.

Jane I bet he did! Really, Mother, you should not invite strangers to the flat. (*She takes the newspaper from the table and puts it on the trolley*)

Mrs Hopkins He was not a stranger. He's the meter man. I know him! He's a very nice man.

Jane I'll take your word for it.

Mrs Hopkins I even showed him the family photo album. He said I was a fine-looking woman in my day.

Jane Mother, you're impossible. I'll leave it here. (*She puts the cap on the sideboard*) I expect he'll be back for it sometime. (*She fusses around her mother, straightening her collar and patting her hair into place*) There now—you are ready for your visitors. (*She has a sudden thought and checks a number on the pad on the trolley*) I think I'll give old Mrs Parks a ring to jog her memory.

Mrs Hopkins (*opening the final card and dropping the envelope to the floor*) H'm, she didn't send me a card. (*She takes off her glasses*)

Jane Probably forgot to post it. (*Dialling a number*) Anyway, it's only along the corridor, seems a waste of a stamp. (*Into the phone*) Hello, hello, Mrs Parks? It's Jane Adams at Number Nine. There's a birthday girl here very much looking forward to seeing you. Hello, are you there? Mrs Parks ... Oh, I just wondered, could you ring the doorbell three times so she knows who it is. (*She looks into the mouthpiece*) H'm, goodbye. (*She replaces the receiver*) Not very talkative this morning.

Mrs Hopkins (*putting her cards on the trolley*) She's never at her best in the mornings. I don't think she eats enough. Spends all her money on food for that blooming cat. Tinned salmon on Sundays. I ask you? Don't know how she does it on her pension.

Jane looks at her, then puts her coat on

Jane I must fly. It's late. (*Pointing to the trolley*) Your tape-recorder is there—your newspaper—and the tray is set in the kitchen. (*Fussing around Mrs Hopkins, she takes an envelope and puts it deliberately in the waste-bin*) And that's for your rubbish! Please use it. Now I must be off. (*She goes to collect her basket*)
Mrs Hopkins My glasses, Jane, where are my glasses?
Jane (*turning with her hands on her hips; exasperatedly*) Round your neck, Mother. (*Sighing*) Anything else?
Mrs Hopkins Oh! I'm sorry. No, dear. And thank you for everything. Bless you.

Jane takes the basket from the chair and then goes and embraces Mrs Hopkins

Jane Be good and take care. I'll see you later. (*She goes to the doorway and then turns*) Mother.
Mrs Hopkins (*looking over her glasses*) Yes, dear?
Jane Promise me you won't let any strangers into the flat. Not unless you know them. Promise?
Mrs Hopkins (*giggling*) I know the meter man! (*Laughing*) Don't worry, Jane, I may be old, but I'm not stupid.

Jane blows a kiss, returned by Mrs Hopkins

Jane exits

Mrs Hopkins gets comfortable, adjusts her collar and cuffs and helps herself to a chocolate, carefully dropping the wrapping into the waste-bin. She puts in the tape and switches it on. The sound of her two grandchildren singing "Happy birthday, dear Granny", followed by much laughter, obviously gives her great pleasure. She dabs a tear with a handkerchief and turns off the tape

The darlings. What a joy. (*She rises and takes the six cards from the trolley to the sideboard, singing "Happy birthday to you" etc. She arranges the cards on the sideboard, counting as she does so*) One—two—three—four——

The doorbell rings, very shrill and long. Mrs Hopkins stands quite still, with two cards in her hand. The doorbell rings again. Mrs Hopkins half turns, slightly bothered. The doorbell rings a third time. Mrs Hopkins, obviously relieved, takes her stick from the back of the chair and puts the two cards on the trolley

> I'm coming, Mrs Parks, I'm coming... (*She goes out to the hall, leaving the door open, and opens the front door*)
>
> *The Visitor steps smartly into the hall. She is about forty with an air of vulgarity. A long fur coat and brassy blonde hair add to her bizarre appearance. She carries a bunch of flowers*

Mrs Hopkins backs into the living-room and the Visitor now stands framed in the doorway

Visitor Happy birthday, Mrs Hopkins. These are for you.
Mrs Hopkins Oh—er—I was expecting my friend Mrs Parks.
Visitor (*holding out the flowers*) For you, Mrs Hopkins...
Mrs Hopkins Flowers for me? But I don't know... (*Suddenly realizing*) Why yes, of course, you'll be from the church. They never forget. Someone always comes on my birthday.
Visitor Aren't you going to ask me in?
Mrs Hopkins Well—er—I—er—yes, of course. How rude of me. Do please come in. My daughter has just left. (*She takes the flowers and puts them on the trolley*) Do sit down, dear. Make yourself comfy.

The Visitor comes into the living-room and closes the door. She stands with her back to it, listening and watching. Her behaviour should be chilling and devious but not enough at this point to arouse Mrs Hopkins' suspicions. Mrs Hopkins goes to the sideboard and pours water from the jug into the vase

> It's so good of them really. I don't go to church anymore, uncomfortable places, don't you think? (*She rubs her bottom*) It's those hard seats. Stops you dropping off I suppose! (*Laughing, she takes the vase to the trolley and sits in her armchair. She throws the paper to the floor and arranges the flowers*) Do sit down, dear. Tell me about yourself. You'll be local, of course?

Visitor (*going to the trolley and picking up a card*) Local? Er—yes, in a manner of speaking. (*She goes to the table, looking at the card, then puts it down*)

Flowers for Mrs Hopkins

Mrs Hopkins We had a house. Not far from here. I miss the garden.

The Visitor wanders up to the bookcase and looks at the photos. Her face hardens. She places the photos face down on the bookcase

I like to potter around. George did all the work. George—my husband. He died. About six months ago. (*Smelling a flower*) It seems longer. What did you say your name was?

Visitor I didn't ...

Mrs Hopkins Oh well—you know mine. (*Pondering*) There's something, something familiar. But I don't think we've met, have we?

Visitor (*lifting a second card from the trolley*) No, we haven't, 'til now ...

Mrs Hopkins (*rising and taking the vase to the sideboard*) As I was saying, it's not quite the same here, in the flat I mean. My daughter wanted me to move in with her and the family (*returning to the armchair she picks up the paper and puts it in the waste-bin*) but I like to be independent. (*She sits*) It's my birthday, you know. Oh, of course you know. The church keep a list. Do please sit down.

Visitor (*standing R of the table*) No-one ever remembers my birthday. (*Holding the card in her right hand she touches the cake frill with her left hand; laughing*) I don't think I remember it myself.

Mrs Hopkins Jane made the cake. I'd cut you a bit, but the children are coming at four. They like to light the candle and see me blow it out. Do you know my friend Mrs Parks? The one who's coming for coffee. She's late.

Visitor (*stroking her fur coat*) Oh yes, I know Mrs Parks. She has a cat. A pale, cream, Persian pussy cat.

Mrs Hopkins That's the one. She's daft about that cat. Sad really. She's no family, you see. (*Turning away*) No-one to be a burden to. I—I just couldn't bear to be a burden. I'd rather be dead.

Visitor (*turning sharply*) Dead!

Mrs Hopkins (*rising; quietly*) Yes. (*Still pondering she walks slowly round the back of the chair*) I've seen you before, there's something—I can't quite place it ...

Visitor (*looking at the card*) Very pretty. (*She opens the card and reads aloud*) "With love from Sue and Kate."

Mrs Hopkins That's my grandchildren. Sue is eight and Kate's nearly eleven. You'd like them, they——
Visitor (*her mood changes*) Would I? (*Slowly she tears up the card and throws the pieces in the air*)
Mrs Hopkins (*shocked*) Why did you do that?
Visitor (*casually*) I don't think I like it anymore.
Mrs Hopkins (*very alarmed, trying to keep calm*) Do you have a family?
Visitor Not anymore. There were lots of us. In a big place. They counted us every night. I didn't like it. So I left ... (*She helps herself to a chocolate. She moves away, almost casually, and embraces herself, stroking each arm of the fur coat*)
Mrs Hopkins (*behind the trolley; very agitatedly*) I—I have a daughter. About your age. (*Deflatedly*) Oh, you know. I told you. (*With a sudden thought*) W—would you like to hear my grandchildren? (*She turns on the tape*)

The Visitor covers her ears with her hands and turns away from Mrs Hopkins, her body shaking

Visitor Turn it off. Stop 'em ...

Mrs Hopkins is terrified. She quickly turns off the tape

    (*Turning to face Mrs Hopkins; spitting out the words*) I hate kids ... all of 'em.
Mrs Hopkins But children, they ... please let me help you. You need help ...
Visitor There were lots of them. Big girls. And boys. I was five. They made me do things. If I didn't they beat me. They burnt me with cigarettes. So I did ... (*she pauses*) ... what they wanted. My mother put me in that place. She left me and never came back. It was very lonely. Have you ever been lonely? (*Smiling smugly*) Mrs Parks was lonely. (*With a change of mood*) Oh, I forgot, this came with the flowers.

Taking a card from her pocket she slowly approaches the almost retreating Mrs Hopkins and hands over the card

Mrs Hopkins (*without her glasses, reading at arm's length*) "From Mrs Parks." (*Confusedly*) But she's coming, you said ... (*Pointing to the flowers*) I don't understand. (*Realizing*) Y—you rang the doorbell three times. How did you know?

Flowers for Mrs Hopkins

The Visitor laughs raucously and removes her fur coat and wig

Visitor (*mimicking Jane's voice*) "Hello, Mrs Parks—there's a birthday girl here at Number Nine—(*she throws the wig and coat over the easy chair*)—could you ring three times, so she knows who it is?" (*Leering*) The stupid bitch.

Mrs Hopkins (*trapped, eyeing the phone and the door*) Oh my God, no. (*Retreating and pointing at the coat*) That coat, that's what I've seen before ...

Visitor Bet your Aunt Fanny you have. Looks better on me than her, don't you think? Anyway, she won't be needing it any more ...

Mrs Hopkins Y—you must be very tired. W—would you like a cup of tea? (*She moves to her armchair, takes her walking stick and makes for the kitchen*) I'll put the kettle on.

The Visitor rushes across and bars Mrs Hopkins' exit. She takes a flick knife from her pocket, and forces Mrs Hopkins to the table. Mrs Hopkins drops her stick and retreats from the knife

Visitor You're going no place, Gran'ma. No place at all.

She pushes the petrified Mrs Hopkins into the dining-chair that faces front. The doorbell rings

Mrs Hopkins (*screaming*) Help——

The scream is barely heard as the Visitor clamps her hand firmly over Mrs Hopkins' mouth. Both women are still, in silence. The knife is held above Mrs Hopkins. The doorbell rings again. Footsteps are finally heard departing. The Visitor, as though to stab Mrs Hopkins, brings the knife down with great force into the middle of the cake

Visitor (*moving away*) Well now, Gran'ma, you got two candles on your cake! Who's a lucky girl then?

Mrs Hopkins (*sobbing*) Meter man, please, please come back ...

Visitor Oh yes, Gran'ma, I nearly forgot. (*Her hand goes slowly into her dress pocket. She pauses momentarily*) I got a present for you. (*Her hand comes quickly out of her pocket holding a cat's tail*) How's that for a nice line in cat's tails? (*Dangling it in front of Mrs Hopkins' face; slowly*) Go on, Gran'ma, stroke it. It's still warm.

Mrs Hopkins (*rising and backing away; aghast*) You did that? How could you? She loved it. That cat was like her child ...

Visitor She don't need a cat anymore. Now, what was you saying about a drink, Gran?

Mrs Hopkins The—the kettle's in the kitchen, through there. There's tea, coffee, and the tray is set.

Visitor (*stroking the cat's tail with relish*) Come on now, Gran'ma. I mean a real drink, a drop of the hard stuff. Where do you keep it, eh?

Mrs Hopkins (*trembling*) I don't know what you mean. If it's alcohol, I don't drink it. There's some orange juice ...

Visitor (*swinging the cat's tail near Mrs Hopkins*) Come off it, Gran'ma. All you old girls keep a drop hidden somewhere. What is it you say: "for medicinal purposes"? (*She laughs, abruptly changes her mood and swings the cat's tail wildly, releasing it in Mrs Hopkins' direction*) I'll find it. (*She goes to the sideboard, opens both doors and sweeps the contents to the floor*) I'll tear this place apart.

Mrs Hopkins I beg of you, please, I'm old. I feel sick ...

Visitor (*losing control completely*) Where is it? You stubborn old cow. (*She clears the top of the sideboard with one swipe. She tries to open the locked drawer*) The key, where's the key?

Mrs Hopkins My daughter has it. There's only private papers and things ...

Visitor (*grabbing Mrs Hopkins' bag from the back of the armchair*) Don't give me that. (*She turns the contents of the bag on to the trolley and holds up the key*) So your daughter has it? What's this, then? (*She unlocks the drawer*)

Mrs Hopkins I told you, it's just some papers, private papers ...

Visitor (*scattering the papers on the floor*) So, what have we got here? (*She takes a small dark bottle from the drawer and removes the screw top*)

Mrs Hopkins (*moving forward*) No, no, not that, please ...

Visitor (*smelling the contents*) Mm—brandy. You crafty old so and so.

Mrs Hopkins (*frantically*) Don't take it, you mustn't, I'll need it. (*More quietly*) For medicinal purposes.

Visitor (*laughing wildly*) Medicinal purposes. Nothing like a drop of the hard stuff, eh, Gran? Down the hatch. (*She gulps down the contents of the bottle, then wipes her mouth on the back of her hand*)

Mrs Hopkins My God—no. (*She is rooted to the spot*) That was—

that was ... (*Realizing*) I must phone, you need help ... (*She moves towards the phone*)

Visitor (*banging down the empty bottle on the trolley*) Stay right where you are, Gran'ma — don't try anything. I gets upset, see. And when I gets upset ... (*She goes to the table and grabs the knife from the cake. Deliberately, she cleans off the icing from the knife with her thumb and forefinger and licks her fingers*) Like a bit of cake, Gran?

Mrs Hopkins (*retreating behind the table*) No, no thank you. I — er — the children are coming — they like to ...

Visitor (*leaning over the table and threatening Mrs Hopkins with the knife; mimicking Jane's voice*) "A birthday girl ... three times ... ring three times." (*Laughing wildly she grabs the edge of the tablecloth and pulls it, and everything on it, to the floor. Moving away; slurred*) Flowers for Mrs Hopkins.

Mrs Hopkins (*bravely and sympathetically*) You need a doctor. I beg of you — before it's too late. That bottle — it was special. For me, when the time came ...

Visitor (*staggering about; almost to herself*) I never had a birthday. I never had no-one. My mother left me — she never came back. It was very lonely. (*Slumping into the armchair and pointing to the bottle*) It was special when the ... (*Clutching her throat, she drops the knife, tries to rise, but fails*) They won't get me now, Gran — will they? They won't ... (*She stiffens, her eyes staring at Mrs Hopkins almost appealingly. Her mouth moves soundlessly*)

Mrs Hopkins (*staggering to the trolley; sobbing*) Oh please God, no. (*Lifting the bottle*) This was for me. (*Her hand goes out to touch the Visitor, but she does not*) She had no-one, not a soul.

Instinctively her hand switches on the tape-recorder. The childish laughter and singing of "Happy birthday, dear Granny" contrasts sharply with the situation. Mrs Hopkins, deeply moved, turns off the tape. The Visitor still sits stiff, her eyes staring at Mrs Hopkins

(*Very emotionally*) You don't need that, Granny Hopkins. (*She drops the bottle, at arm's length into the waste-bin*)

Her arm is still outstretched as —

BLACK-OUT

FURNITURE AND PROPERTY LIST

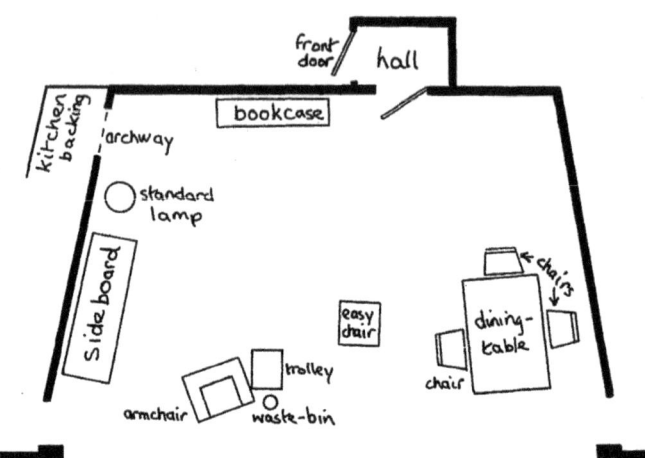

Further dressing may be added at the director's direction

On stage: Sideboard. *In locked drawer:* private papers, dark coloured screw-top bottle containing small amount of liquid. *In unlocked drawer:* cutlery, paper napkins. *In cupboard:* cups, saucers. *On top:* empty flower vase, tray with bottle of orange juice and glass
Standard lamp
Bookcase. *On shelves:* books. *On top shelf:* framed photos of children, biscuit tin
Dining-table. *On it:* tablecloth
3 dining-chairs
Easy chair. *Under it:* man's cap
Armchair. *Hanging on back:* **Mrs Hopkins'** handbag containing key to sideboard drawer, etc.
Trolley. *On lower shelf:* phone pad, magazines. *On upper shelf:* phone, tape-recorder
Waste-bin

Flowers for Mrs Hopkins

Off stage: Hoover **(Mrs Hopkins)**
Birthday cake with 1 candle and frill wrapped in tin foil on a plate, shopping basket with packet of biscuits, newspaper, tape, gift-wrapped parcel containing chocolates, cardigan and 2 birthday cards in envelopes **(Jane)**
Jug of water, empty shopping basket **(Jane)**
Mail bag containing letters, bills, 3 cards addressed to **Mrs Hopkins**, gift-wrapped parcel containing soap and birthday card in envelope **(Postie)**
Wrapped bunch of flowers **(Visitor)**

Personal: **Mrs Hopkins:** walking stick, reading glasses on chain round neck, duster and hanky in cardigan pocket
Jane: wristwatch
Visitor: long fur coat with birthday card in envelope in pocket, blonde wig, "cat's tail" and flick knife in dress pocket

LIGHTING PLOT

Interior. The same scene throughout

To open: General overall lighting

Cue 1   **Mrs Hopkins** remains with her arm outstretched   (Page 13)
Black-out

EFFECTS PLOT

Cue 1	**Mrs Hopkins** switches on hoover *Hoover effect*	(Page 1)
Cue 2	**Jane** switches off hoover *Cut hoover effect*	(Page 1)
Cue 3	**Jane:** "... to watch the roads." *Sound of whistling followed by shrill doorbell ring*	(Page 3)
Cue 4	**Jane:** "... anymore letters?" *Shrill doorbell ring*	(Page 4)
Cue 5	**Mrs Hopkins** switches on tape *Start tape of children singing*	(Page 7)
Cue 6	**Mrs Hopkins** switches off tape *Snap off tape*	(Page 7)
Cue 7	**Mrs Hopkins:** "One—two—three—four——" *Doorbell rings shrill and long. Pause, doorbell 2nd time. Pause, doorbell 3rd time*	(Page 7)
Cue 8	**Mrs Hopkins** switches on tape *Snap on tape*	(Page 10)
Cue 9	**Mrs Hopkins** switches off tape *Snap off tape*	(Page 10)
Cue 10	**Visitor** pushes **Mrs Hopkins** into dining-chair *Doorbell*	(Page 11)
Cue 11	**Mrs Hopkins** (*screaming*): "Help——" *Pause, then doorbell rings, finally followed by departing footsteps*	(Page 11)
Cue 12	**Mrs Hopkins** switches on tape *Snap on tape*	(Page 13)
Cue 13	**Mrs Hopkins** switches off tape *Snap off tape*	(Page 13)

www.ingramcontent.com/pod-product-compliance
Ingram Content Group UK Ltd.
Pitfield, Milton Keynes, MK11 3LW, UK
UKHW021859060225
454771UK00026B/377